S0-BOE-935

THINK BEFORE YOU ACT

IMPULSE CONTROL

SARAH MACHAJEWSKI

PowerKiDS press™

NEW YORK

Published in 2020 by The Rosen Publishing Group, Inc.
29 East 21st Street, New York, NY 10010

Copyright © 2020 by The Rosen Publishing Group, Inc.

All rights reserved. No part of this book may be reproduced in any form without permission in writing from the publisher, except by a reviewer.

Editor: Rachel Gintner
Cover Design: Michael Flynn

Photo Credits: Cover Alistair Berg/DigitalVision/Getty Images; cover, pp. 1, 3–4, 6, 8, 10, 12, 14–16, 18, 20, 22–24 TairA/Shutterstock.com; p. 4 https://en.wikipedia.org/wiki/Roy_Baumeister#/media/File:Roy_Baumeister.jpg; p. 5 Image Source/DigitalVision/Getty Images; p. 6 https://en.wikipedia.org/wiki/Carl_Lange_(physician)#/media/File:Carl_Georg_Lange_by_Peter_Most.jpg; p. 7 Alena Ozerova/Shutterstock.com; p. 9 Jeff Greenberg/Universal Images Group/Getty Images; p. 11 Viktoria Alisevich/Shutterstock.com; p. 13 iofoto/Shutterstock.com; p. 14 Elena Nichizhenova/Shutterstock.com; p. 15 ANURAK PONGPATIMET/Shutterstock.com; p. 17 zentradyi3ell/Shutterstock.com; p. 19 Olena Yakobchuk/Shutterstock.com; p. 21 Syda Productions/Shutterstock.com; p. 22 Daboost/Shutterstock.com.

Cataloging-in-Publication Data

Names: Machajewski, Sarah.
Title: Think before you act: impulse control / Sarah Machajewski.
Description: New York : PowerKids Press, 2020. | Series: Spotlight on social and emotional learning | Includes glossary and index.
Identifiers: ISBN 9781725302105 (pbk.) | ISBN 9781725302297 (library bound) | ISBN 9781725302204 (6pack)
Subjects: LCSH: Self-control--Juvenile literature. | Emotions in children--Juvenile literature. | Control (Psychology)--Juvenile literature.
Classification: LCC BF632.M33 2020 | DDC 153.8--dc23

Manufactured in the United States of America

CPSIA Compliance Information: Batch #CSPK19. For further information contact Rosen Publishing, New York, New York at 1-800-237-9932.

CONTENTS

"CONTROL YOURSELF!" 4

YOU'RE IN CONTROL 6

ACTING ON EMOTION 8

STOP AND THINK 10

LABEL YOUR FEELINGS 12

KEEP A JOURNAL 14

SET GOALS 16

COUNT TO 10 18

MORE STRATEGIES TO PRACTICE 20

KEEP TRYING! 22

GLOSSARY 23

INDEX 24

PRIMARY SOURCE LIST 24

WEBSITES 24

CHAPTER ONE

"CONTROL YOURSELF!"

"Control yourself!" As a kid, you've probably heard this command a lot. Whether you're told to eat just one piece of candy or told to keep your hands to yourself, knowing how to control yourself is an important part of growing up.

Controlling your behavior isn't always easy, but it's a skill everyone needs to have. Why? Because controlling yourself allows you to think before you act, which gives you the chance to take more time and do the right thing. Being in control of your emotions helps you have good **relationships** with your parents, friends, and teachers because they can communicate more clearly with you when you're calm. Controlling yourself also helps you **navigate** any situation, no matter how silly or **stressful** it may be. When you think first, you can prepare for almost anything!

Roy Baumeister is a top **psychologist** who has studied **impulse** control.

Picture yourself at the grocery store. Try buying only a few pieces of candy, even if you may want more. This is one way to practice controlling your choices and behavior.

CHAPTER TWO

YOU'RE IN CONTROL

One special quality of being human is that you can control a lot of what you do. Move forward, move backward, blink twice, smile or frown—you can control these actions. You can choose how much you want to eat for dinner. You can put on a yellow shirt or a gray sweater, or both. You can even decide to read your favorite book five times in a row. It's easy to see how you can control these things. Did you know you can control what's going on inside you, too?

The feelings you have inside your head and your heart are called your emotions. You feel emotions because of what you experience, like seeing your friend and feeling happy or losing something and feeling sad. Emotions are a part of being human.

Carl Lange was a Danish psychologist who constructed **theories** about where human emotions come from.

CHAPTER THREE

ACTING ON EMOTION

The way you feel inside may make you want to act a certain way. Have you ever wanted to scream when you're excited or hit something when you're **frustrated**? These feelings are called urges, or impulses.

Everyone experiences these feelings and they're completely normal. However, just because the feeling is there doesn't mean you should act on it. For example, you wouldn't scream in a library—you know it's a place to be quiet. And you know that hitting things may cause yourself or others to be hurt. Being able to control impulses such as these is called self-regulation. You may also hear it called self-discipline or self-control. Whatever you call it, this skill will help you in many ways. It will help you stay happy, have good relationships with people, and spend more time on important things, such as school.

Self-discipline is a lifelong skill. You'll use it at home, at school, and when you're out and about in the world.

You are now in the

silent study zone

CHAPTER FOUR

STOP AND THINK

Impulses can be really hard to control. Sometimes, the **desire** to blurt things out feels stronger than knowing you should raise your hand to speak. Or maybe it feels good to eat another cookie, but your mom or dad told you to have only one. You can learn to control these feelings, and it will get easier the more you practice. There are a lot of ways to learn self-control, but they all have this in common: you must stop and think before you act.

Try it out for yourself. Consider how you're feeling now. Then, think about the following questions. What does this feeling make you want to do? Why? Should you act on your feelings right now? Why or why not? How would doing so affect others? Do you still want to act, or do you feel differently now?

A famous study done by Walter Mischel is called "the marshmallow test." **Researchers** placed marshmallows on a plate and told young kids they could eat one right away, or two if they waited. This tested their ability to self-regulate.

CHAPTER FIVE

LABEL YOUR FEELINGS

Notice how stopping to think gives you time to consider your situation. When you take this time, you can think clearly and work on avoiding anxiety. Another reason why thinking first is **critical** is because it can help you understand what you're really feeling.

It's often easy to mistake one feeling for another. The way you act may not always represent how you feel. It's hard to know how to feel better if you don't know what's going on inside. In these situations, a good **strategy** is to label your feelings. This means you should give your feelings a name. Try something simple, such as, "I feel mad."

Naming your emotions helps you gain control over them. By doing this, you have a tool that will help you resist your urge to act on that feeling.

Get in the habit of naming your feelings. You can say the names out loud or write them down on a piece of paper.

CHAPTER SIX

KEEP A JOURNAL

Whether it's doing your homework, completing chores, or spending time on an important task, you probably have a lot of responsibilities. Staying on track is important and self-regulation will help you do it.

One way to make this process easier is to keep a journal. You can use your journal to keep track of your day or week. Write down your tasks and any goals you have. When these things are written down in one place, you can go back and reread what you've written. This will help you learn to manage your time and your attention.

Self-regulation involves skills such as planning, setting important markers, managing your time, and sticking to your goals.

Another benefit of keeping a journal is that it will allow you to see your progress. Did you forget any tasks? Did you meet all your goals? Reviewing and reflecting will help you understand what worked and what didn't.

CHAPTER SEVEN

SET GOALS

Think about something you really want to accomplish. What will it take to do it? It may take a lot of control, attention, and **motivation**. These things are self-control skills.

Setting and sticking to goals is a great way to grow these skills. Here's how to get started.

Step 1: Choose your goal. Make sure it's something you want to do. That will help you stay interested.

Step 2: Think about the "why." Why is this goal important to you? How will meeting it help you?

Step 3: Break the goal into smaller steps. Meeting small progress points will make a big goal seem less scary.

Step 4: Plan ahead. Think about everything it will take to meet your goal. Learn what you have to do to stay in control. Prepare yourself to succeed!

My goals

1

2

3

4

Use your journal to write down your goals, your plan of attack, and the small steps you can take to meet those goals. Writing it all down can help you see the big picture.

CHAPTER EIGHT

COUNT TO 10

Sometimes staying in control can be as simple as counting to 10. This is an age-old strategy that really works.

When you get upset or excited about something, it's easy to do or say the first thing that comes to mind. Part of controlling your impulses is thinking before you act. Counting to 10 gives you the time you need to think. It will help you stay calm and in control of your emotions. It also helps because your mind gets a break from thinking about whatever it is that's causing you to react.

When you feel the urge to act, pause. Take a deep breath. Say the numbers "1…2…3…" and so on until you reach 10. See how this short pause helped you stay in control? Now, you can act or speak with a clear head.

Ten seconds may be enough time to help you stay calm and in control. However, you can take this same approach for longer periods of time. If you feel like your emotions are running high, give yourself a day to think about what you should do.

CHAPTER NINE

MORE STRATEGIES TO PRACTICE

One reason you may struggle to control your impulses is because the urge to act takes over your ability to self-regulate. It's OK! Many people, even adults, experience this struggle. But, it's important to think before you act.

Psychologists sometimes advise thinking about the future in every situation. This can help you change your behavior so that, when you're in certain situations, you know well ahead of time how you need to act. This will even give you time to practice!

Start by naming a place or situation where you know your impulses always take over, such as at school. Picture yourself in your classroom. Do you know how you're expected to behave? If so, practice those behaviors. For example, try sitting still in your seat. Raise your hand and practice staying quiet. Now you know exactly what to do!

Practicing ahead of time will help you be on your best behavior in school. This will allow you and your classmates to pay attention and stay calm.

21

CHAPTER TEN

KEEP TRYING!

If there's one important thing to remember about self-regulation, it's this: developing this skill takes time and patience. There's a good chance you won't get it right on your first try, and that's OK. But if you're **committed** to learning this skill, you'll definitely succeed.

Success starts by reviewing all of the strategies you've learned in this book. Take the time to practice your behavior before you're in a situation. Make your goal chart and write in your journal every day. Try counting to 10 the next time you feel the urge to act. These strategies really work!

There's one more thing you can do as you practice your impulse control—ask for help. When you tell someone what's going on, they can help you succeed, and you'll make progress together. You'll be on your way to thinking first in no time at all!

GLOSSARY

commit (kuh-MIHT) To make a promise to do something.

critical (KRIH-tuh-kuhl) Of great importance.

desire (dih-ZY-uhr) The feeling of wanting something or to do something.

frustrated (FRUH-stray-tuhd) Feeling angered or let down.

impulse (IHM-puhls) A quick feeling or desire to take action.

motivation (moh-tuh-VAY-shun) The feeling of wanting to get something done.

navigate (nah-vuh-GAYT) To find one's way.

psychologist (sy-KAH-luh-jist) A person who studies psychology, or the science or study of the mind and behavior.

relationship (ree-LAY-shun-ship) A connection with someone else.

researcher (ree-SUHR-chuhr) Someone who does research, or careful study to find new knowledge.

strategy (STRAA-tuh-jee) A plan of action to achieve a goal.

stressful (STRES-ful) Causing strong feelings of worry.

theory (THEER-ee) An idea suggested or presented as possibly true but that's not known or proven to be true.

INDEX

A
anxiety, 12

B
Baumeister, Roy, 4
behavior, 4, 5, 20, 21, 22

C
choices, 5

E
emotions, 4, 6, 12, 18

F
feelings, 6, 8, 10, 12

G
goals, 14, 15, 16, 17, 22

J
journal, 14, 15, 17, 22

L
Lange, Carl, 6

M
Mischel, Walter, 10
motivation, 16

P
psychologist, 4, 6, 20

R
relationships, 4, 8
responsibilities, 14

S
self-control, 8, 10, 16
self-discipline, 8
self-regulation, 8, 10, 14, 15, 20, 22
strategy, 12, 18, 20, 22

T
time, 4, 12, 14, 15, 18, 20, 21, 22

U
urges, 8, 18, 20

PRIMARY SOURCE LIST

Page 4
Dr. Roy F. Baumeister, lecturing at ZURICH.MINDS, 2011. Photograph. ZURICH.MINDS. January 1, 2012.

Page 6
Carl Henrik Lange (1834–1900), Danish physician and psychologist. Photograph. Peter Most. Copenhagen, Denmark.

WEBSITES

Due to the changing nature of Internet links, PowerKids Press has developed an online list of websites related to the subject of this book. This site is updated regularly. Please use this link to access the list: www.powerkidslinks.com/SSEL/think